PIANO/VOCAL SELECTIONS

The Addams Family

Stuart Oken   Roy Furman   Michael Leavitt   Five Cent Productions
Stephen Schuler   Decca Theatricals   Scott M. Delman   Stuart Ditsky   Terry Allen Kramer   Stephanie P. McClelland
James L. Nederlander   Eva Price   Jam Theatricals/Mary Lu Roffe   Pittsburgh CLO/Gutterman-Swinsky
Vivek Tiwary/Gary Kaplan   The Weinstein Company/Clarence, LLC   Adam Zotovich/Tribe Theatricals

by Special Arrangement with
Elephant Eye Theatrical

present

Nathan Lane   Bebe Neuwirth

in

The Addams Family
A NEW MUSICAL

Book by
Marshall Brickman & Rick Elice

Music and Lyrics by
Andrew Lippa

Based on Characters Created by
Charles Addams

Starring
**Terrence Mann   Carolee Carmello
Kevin Chamberlin**

With
**Jackie Hoffman   Zachary James   Adam Riegler
Wesley Taylor** and **Krysta Rodriguez**

**Merwin Foard   Jim Borstelmann   Erick Buckley   Colin Cunliffe   Rachel de Benedet
Valerie Fagan   Matthew Gumley   Fred Inkley   Morgan James   Clark Johnsen   Barrett Martin
Jessica Lea Patty   Liz Ramos   Samantha Sturm   Charlie Sutton   Aléna Watters**

Lighting Design by	Sound Design by	Puppetry by
Natasha Katz	**Acme Sound Partners**	**Basil Twist**
Hair Design by	Make-up Design by	Special Effects by
Tom Watson	**Angelina Avallone**	**Gregory Meeh**

Orchestrations	Music Director	Dance Arrangements	Vocal Arrangements & Incidental Music
Larry Hochman	**Mary-Mitchell Campbell**	**August Eriksmoen**	**Andrew Lippa**

Casting	Press Representative	Marketing	Music Coordinator
Telsey + Company	**The Publicity Office**	**Type A Marketing**	**Michael Keller**

Production Supervisor	Production Management	General Management
Beverley Randolph	**Aurora Productions**	**101 Productions, Ltd.**

Creative Consultant
Jerry Zaks

Choreography by
Sergio Trujillo

Directed and Designed by
Phelim McDermott & Julian Crouch

The Addams Family artwork © Charles Addams, used with
permission of the Tee and Charles Addams Foundation.

ISBN 978-1-4234-9580-2

HAL•LEONARD®
CORPORATION
7777 W. Bluemound Rd. P.O. Box 13819 Milwaukee, WI 53213

In Australia Contact:
Hal Leonard Australia Pty. Ltd.
4 Lentara Court
Cheltenham, Victoria, 3192 Australia
Email: ausadmin@halleonard.com.au

Visit Hal Leonard Online at
www.halleonard.com

ANDREW LIPPA's acclaimed score to *The Addams Family* was nominated for a Tony® Award and two Drama Desk Awards and was recorded by Decca Broadway. The original Broadway cast featured Nathan Lane and Bebe Neuwirth with a book by Marshall Brickman and Rick Elice (*Jersey Boys*). In 2008, Mr. Lippa wrote the music for the Broadway production of Aaron Sorkin's ("The West Wing," *A Few Good Men*) play *The Farnsworth Invention*, directed by Des McAnuff. *Asphalt Beach* (music and lyrics) was premiered at Northwestern University by the American Music Theatre Project in October, 2006. *The Wild Party* (book/music/lyrics) was given its world premiere in 2000 at the Manhattan Theater Club in New York City. *The Wild Party* won the Outer Critics Circle Award for Best Off-Broadway Musical of the season, and Mr. Lippa won the 2000 Drama Desk Award for Best Music. 2004 saw the premiere of *A Little Princess* (book and lyrics by Brian Crawley) at Theatreworks in Palo Alto, CA. In 1999 he contributed three new songs to the Broadway version of *You're A Good Man, Charlie Brown* (including "My New Philosophy" for Tony® Award Winner Kristin Chenoweth) and created all new arrangements. He wrote the music and co-wrote the book (with Tom Greenwald) for *john & jen*, which premiered in New York City in 1995 at The Lamb's Theater.

Mr. Lippa is proud to have been music director for Kristin Chenoweth since 1999 for many of her concerts. He conducted/played her sold-out shows at the Metropolitan Opera House in NYC in 2007, at Carnegie Hall in 2004, and at the Donmar Warehouse in London in 2002. He has conducted the San Francisco, Chicago, and St. Louis Symphony Orchestras for Ms. Chenoweth, among others. Additionally, he is an accomplished singer having been heard in many venues in New York and, in 2005, as a guest artist at the Adelaide Cabaret Convention in Adelaide, Australia.

Recordings include Julia Murney's CD, *I'm Not Waiting* (producer, 3 songs), *The Wild Party* (RCA Victor) which he also produced, *You're A Good Man, Charlie Brown* (RCA Victor) which earned him a GRAMMY Award® nomination, *The Addams Family* (released June 8, 2010) and *john & jen* (Fynsworth Alley) which he associate produced. Jazz phenom Peter Cincotti recorded the song "Raise The Roof" on his CD titled *On The Moon* (Phil Ramone, producer). In addition, Mr. Lippa produced the original cast recording of *Bat Boy* for RCA Victor and his singing voice can be heard on *The Sondheim Album* (Fynsworth Alley) and *If I Sing* (PS Classics). Vocal selections from *The Wild Party* and *john & jen* are published by Hal Leonard and licensed by MTI.

Awards include a Tony® and a GRAMMY nomination, the Gilman/Gonzalez-Falla Theater Foundation Award, ASCAP's Richard Rodgers/New Horizons Award, The Drama Desk, The Outer Critics Circle, and 2nd place for the Alice B. Deucey Award for all-around outstanding fifth-grader (lost to Cynthia Fink). Additionally, Mr. Lippa is part of the Emmy® Award-winning composing team that created the music for the Nickelodeon TV series *The Wonder Pets*. Memberships include ASCAP, Actor's Equity, the AF of M and The Dramatists Guild.

A graduate of the University of Michigan, Mr. Lippa serves on the council of The Dramatists Guild and was the High Holiday cantor at Congregation Beth Tikvah in Richmond, British Columbia for 10 years from 1998–2007. He was born in Leeds, England but grew up in suburban Detroit.

www.andrewlippa.com

© 2009 dirty sugar photography

Andrew Lippa thanks:

Lynn Mizzy Jonas, Next Decade Entertainment, Monica Corton and Stu Kantor

Rick Walters, Mark Carlstein and everyone at Hal Leonard

Chris Roberts, Brian Drutman and Decca Broadway.

Larry Hochman, August Eriksmoen, Jim Abbott, Michael Keller, Annie Kaye and Doug Houston, Chris Fe Damien Bassman, Tim Rosser, Ben Krauss

Mark Sendroff and everyone at Sendroff & Baruch

Olivier Sultan and my team at CAA

Stuart Oken and Roy Furman

This volume is dedicated to:

Mary-Mitchell Campbell—music director nonpareil

Will Van Dyke—my other left hand

And especially, David Bloch—the source of all that is right in my life

WHEN YOU'RE AN ADDAMS

Music and Lyrics by
ANDREW LIPPA

*Men sing where written these two bars

PULLED

Music and Lyrics by
ANDREW LIPPA

WEDNESDAY:
I don't have a sun-ny dis-po-si-tion. I'm not known for be-ing too a-mused. My de-mean-or's locked in one po-si-tion. See my face? I'm en-thused. Sud-den-ly, how-ev-er, I've been

pulled in a new di-rec-tion. Through my pain-ful pur-suit ___ some-how

bird-ies took root. ___ All the things I de-test-ed im-pos-si-bly cute. ___ God!

What do I do? ___ Moth-er al-ways said, "Be kind to

stran-gers." But she does-n't know what they de-stroy.

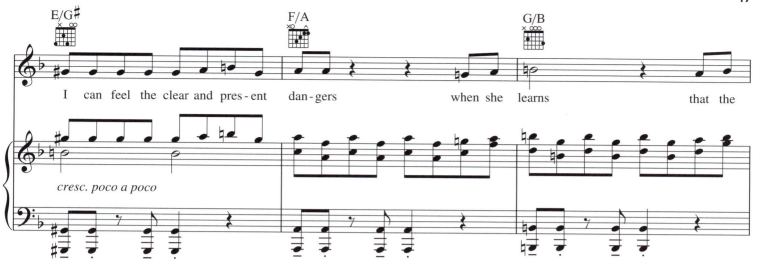

I can feel the clear and pres-ent dan-gers when she learns that the

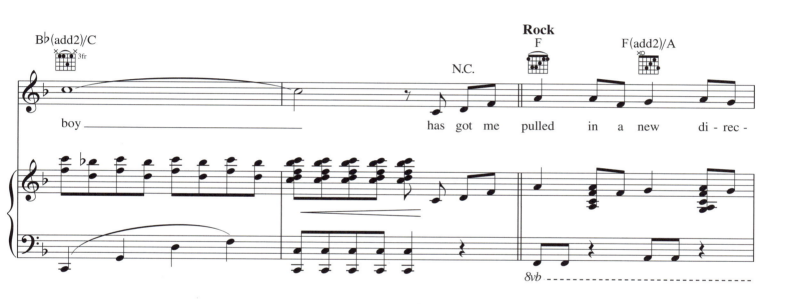

boy _____ has got me pulled in a new di-rec-

-tion, but I think I like ___ it. I think I like _

PUGSLY:

Aaah! _

(torture crank)

That was good, that was good.

ONE NORMAL NIGHT

Music and Lyrics by
ANDREW LIPPA

MORTICIA

Music and Lyrics by
ANDREW LIPPA

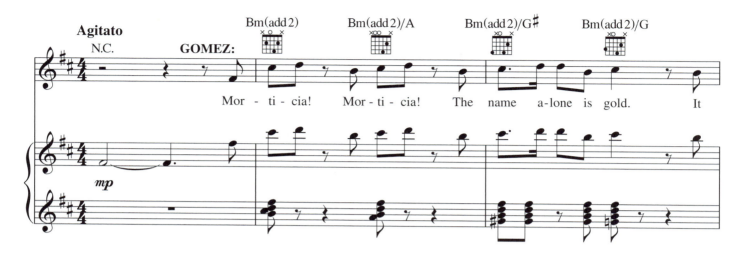

Mor - ti - cia! Mor - ti - cia! The name a-lone is gold. It

speaks of death and la-bored breath, not fears of grow-ing old. If I could stop the clock right now to

make a sim-ple wish, the on - ly wish that I would wish is Tish, Tish,

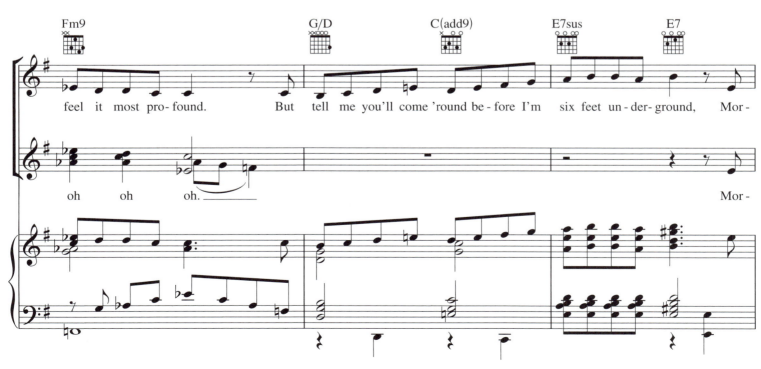

GOMEZ: *Niiice...*

ti - cia!

If I love you and you love me then

lose this fresh fa - cade. My in - gé - nue, I'll help you to a - void the fir - ing squad. And

life will be, for us you'll see, in - ter - mi - na - bly odd!

There's not a

ANCESTORS:

Mor - ti - cia! _____

WHAT IF

Music and Lyrics by
ANDREW LIPPA

WAITING

Music and Lyrics by
ANDREW LIPPA

Moderately, melodramatically

ALICE:

Ah _____ Ah _____

Slower

Ah! _____

A wom-an waits for mar-riage, a wom-an waits for chil-dren. She

JUST AROUND THE CORNER

Music and Lyrics by
ANDREW LIPPA

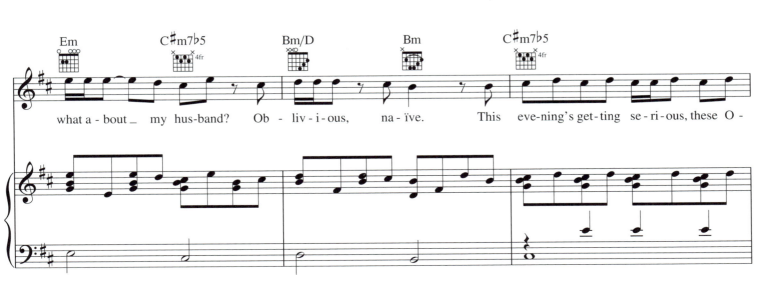

Morticia sings one octave lower.

58

THE MOON AND ME

Music and Lyrics by
ANDREW LIPPA

HAPPY/SAD

Music and Lyrics by
ANDREW LIPPA

CRAZIER THAN YOU

Music and Lyrics by
ANDREW LIPPA

cra - zi - er____ than you! __ That's just the o - ver - view. __ So,

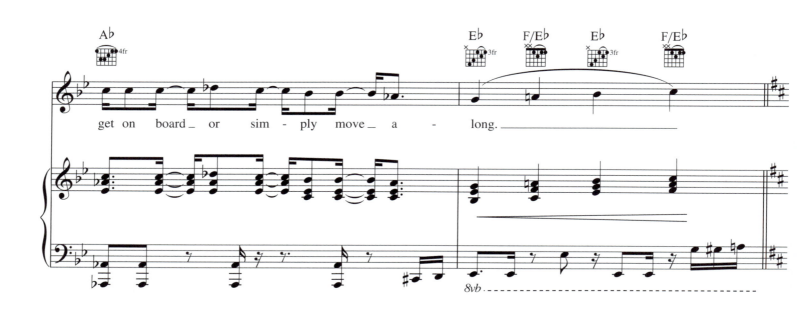

get on board __ or sim - ply move __ a - long. ____

WEDNESDAY:

And yet __ I tru - ly love __ you.

LUCAS:

I'm not _____ im - pul - sive.

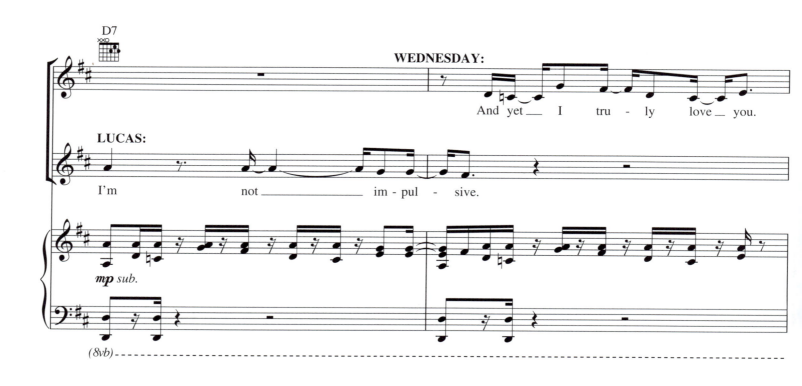

mp sub.

(8vb)

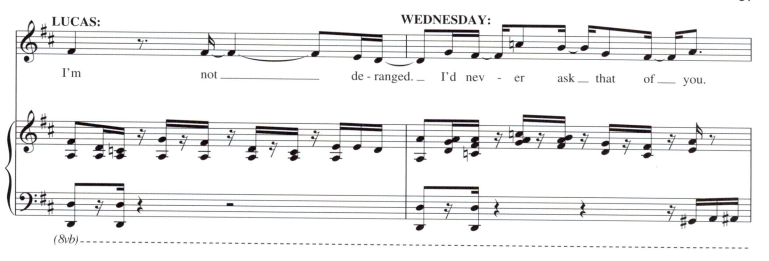

LUCAS:
I'm not de - ranged.

WEDNESDAY:
I'd nev - er ask that of you.

LUCAS:
But in this mo - ment

I feel I'm changed. I wan - na

LET'S NOT TALK ABOUT ANYTHING ELSE BUT LOVE

Music and Lyrics by
ANDREW LIPPA

IN THE ARMS

Music and Lyrics by
ANDREW LIPPA

squid I was saved and born a-new. She saw my

soul. She took con-trol and fi-n'lly I _____ can stom-ach

ALICE:

She saw your soul. She took con-trol.

su-shi. But my dear, now it's clear: My love for you is

Oh, Mal! Big Mal! My love for you is

LIVE BEFORE WE DIE

Music and Lyrics by
ANDREW LIPPA

THE ADDAMS FAMILY THEME

Music and Lyrics by
VIC MIZZY

Moderately

Finger snap

They're creep-y and they're kook-y, mys-te-ri-ous and spook-y, they're al-to-geth-er ook-y, the Ad-dams Fam-i-ly. Their house is a mu-se-um, where

"The show's pedigree is excellent. Composer Andrew Lippa proves as adept with lyrics as with tunes. The songs really shine!"

—John Simon, *Bloomberg News*

"The cleverest lines are in Andrew Lippa's songs, whose melodies are pastiches of tangos and fandangos, vaudeville numbers, patter songs, a killer torch number and more."

—Hedy Weiss, *Chicago Sun-Times*

The Addams Family Original Broadway Cast Recording is available on *Decca Broadway*

www.deccabroadway.com